PUEBLO POTTERY
OF THE NEW MEXICO INDIANS

A MUSEUM OF NEW MEXICO PRESS GUIDEBOOK

PUEBLO POTTERY

OF THE NEW MEXICO INDIANS:

Ever Constant,
Ever Changing

BY BETTY TOULOUSE

Museum of New Mexico Press • Santa Fe

Photography: Color photography by Nancy Warren. Individual pieces photographed by Art Taylor. All pots shown are from the collections in the Musuem of New Mexico. The historic pictures at the beginning of each section featuring noted Pueblo potters Julian and Maria Martinez were made by Wyatt Davis.

Book design by Betsy James

Fifth Printing

ISBN: 0-89013-091-4
Library of Congress Catalog Card Number 77-71898

CONTENTS

INTRODUCTION

We see and know relatively little about the almost boundless creativity of the ancient and recent Pueblo Indian potters—even though archaeologists have devoted years to classifying potsherds into innumerable impersonal pottery types, and ethnologists and art historians have done likewise with the relatively few surviving pots made during the past two or three centuries.

Our ignorance becomes increasingly evident when, as a result of the revitalization of pottery making among the Pueblos, public clamor has risen, demanding more information about potters, pottery, people and events that influenced them, and how they all came to be such integral factors in the long and fascinating history of the Southwest.

Museums display Pueblo pottery, collectors prize it, scholars study it, and, perhaps most importantly, the Pueblo potters themselves also research it. Whether the pottery is in the form of potsherds from ancient ruins or modern pueblo dumping grounds, or is a large collection of vessels, such as the one at the Museum of New Mexico, it all constitutes a stimulating reservoir of ideas for the Pueblo potters who may spend hours sorting over potsherds or looking at museum shelves full of pots, sketching, touching, and remembering. From such research may come new pots to be entered at the Eight Northern Pueblos Annual Artist and Craftsman Show, the Gallup Inter-tribal Indian Ceremonial, or the Santa Fe Indian Market for awards and sale; pots which reflect both innovations and long-standing traditions of design, vessel form, and technique.

Coupled with increasing interest in actually seeing Pueblo pottery on display is more frequent public referral to long out-of-print books and articles on the subject by such pioneer Southwesternists as H. P. Mera, Kenneth M. Chapman, Ruth Bunzel, and Carl E. Guthe, all of whom wrote about Pueblo pottery making more than forty years ago, and many of whose works are being reprinted. With a life that witnessed Pueblo pottery making for over sixty-five years, Kenneth M. Chapman's study, *The Pottery of San Ildefonso Pueblo* (1970), provides a link between the earlier generation of writers and the new generation which includes Francis H. Harlow, Larry Frank, Betty LeFree, and the author of this book, Betty Toulouse.

Drawing on her long associations with both the Pueblo potters and the various museums and foundations which brought together the large collections on which she bases her discussions, Mrs. Toulouse provides an historical perspective that no other individual could. Her familiarity with Pueblo pottery began in the mid-1930s when she worked with H. P. Mera at the Laboratory of Anthropology, and it continued to grow during successive, and sometimes simultaneous, stints as curator of collections with the Indian Arts Fund, the School of American Research, and the Museum of New Mexico over the next forty-odd years.

Although the Pueblo potter may most assuredly trace her or his craft back through twenty-four centuries of linear development within the Southwest—and 1500 years earlier in the source areas of the craft in Mexico, Mrs. Toulouse amply illustrates that Pueblo pottery making has always been responding to new and ever-changing stimuli both from within the Pueblo culture and outside.

Early in this century pottery making among the Pueblos seemed destined for extinction, but it was sustained and rejuvenated through the combined efforts of numerous concerned individuals and organizations, various calendric crafts events, and the dedication of a relatively small number of potters. The names of some of the latter are well-known, but others of equal diligence and creativity have, regrettably, remained anonymous—just as countless generations of their predecessors must.

It is unlikely that today's Pueblo potters will remain anonymous. It is hard to conceive of a period in the Pueblo past when the potters were as vital, innovative, and productive as they are today. Far from becoming extinct, Pueblo pottery making continues to be the most distinctive, versatile, and long-lived craft of any North American Indian group.

Stewart L. Peckham, Director
Division of Anthropology
Museum of New Mexico

1 · PROLOGUE TO THE NEW CREATIVITY

THE CLAY came from the native earth, and comes today from the native earth. It is fired into an enduring creation of the hand of man—practical, beautiful, expressive of a special culture and its special ways.

Pueblo Indian pottery from the American Southwest is recognized around the world for its excellence and uniqueness, its marvelous variety and links to tradition.

Pottery has been with the Pueblos as long as they have existed as a specific people. At prehistoric village sites, it is the broken pottery remains which present archaeologists and historians with the clearest record of the activities and movements of the people, their numbers, and their contacts with other groups. Potters of the present use ancient pottery sherds which they have collected to give proper temper to their new ceramic works.

Today, pottery is the hallmark of the living Pueblos, and beyond the cultural upheavals of the present era, pottery will no doubt endure as a symbol of Pueblo vitality and cultural identity.

Choose any specific area in which Pueblo pottery was produced and choose any specific time during the history of pottery making and you will find that only a very few forms and design schemes were in vogue at that place and at that time.

Choose again the same area but a different time at a later date and you will find that the forms and design schemes are different from the earlier ones—sometimes minimally, sometimes radically. Whether or not the changes are slight or great, there are almost always design elements of the near past or distant past which were retained intact, adapted with modifications, or revived from the styles of years gone by.

The changes were brought about by events of one kind or another which affected the lives of the potters and which in time were reflected in the form and design of the pottery produced in that area.

Choose the northerly part of New Mexico as the area, and choose the greater part of the nineteenth century. The events which began to take place in this area at this time were many and did indeed have an effect on form and design of pottery produced in this area from then until the present moment.

1821: OPENING OF THE SANTA FE TRAIL

Captain William Becknell, assisted by four companions, freighted goods by packhorse from Missouri to New Mexico. The next year, he left Franklin, Missouri, with twenty-one men and three wagons, turning the first wagon wheels over the thick buffalo grass of what was to become the Santa Fe Trail.

This event had a lasting effect on the pottery of the northern New Mexico pueblos. Some of the traders who came over the Santa Fe Trail between 1821 and 1880 were dealers in commercially manufactured kitchen wares, tin pails, and enamelware containers which eventually took the place of much of the Pueblo-made pottery wares in the homes of the region.

An Acoma Pueblo pot dated 1870.

Examples of Zuni pottery collected in 1885.

COMING OF THE RAILROADS

1880   The Atchison, Topeka, and Santa Fe Railroad reached Santa Fe, New Mexico on February 9, 1880.

1880   The Denver and Rio Grande Western Railroad main line to the south reached Española, New Mexico, a number of months later.

1885   The main line of the D&RGW was extended to Santa Fe.

The railroads carried on in an ever-greater volume the freighting business which had originally come over the Santa Fe Trail, bringing more replacements for native-made pottery, and also the vacationing visitor—the "tourist"—who was fascinated with the Indian. Tourists wanted souvenirs made by the Indians. The Indians were willing to supply the souvenirs because it meant an income, however small, which was very much needed by the potters and their families. From 1870 on there had been a gradual change in climatic conditions with a gradual decline in rainfall. Since the Pueblo people subsisted basically on dry farming, the yield from their fields was not as large as it had been in years gone by, and animals sought for food had retreated to higher elevations. The monetary system of the white man thus began to make more and more sense.

1880-1900: PUEBLO POTTERY FORMS AND DESIGNS

Early in the period between 1880 and 1900 some traditional styles in pottery continued to be made at a number of pueblos, but later in the period, due to the tourist demand, the "curio" wares

14

came into being. In a sense, this amounted to a revival of pottery making in some areas and a change of style in other areas. However, it was not a return to pottery making as it had been before the appearance of the traders. This resurgence of pottery was in the form of small items made in the shapes familiar to the easterner—bowls with handles, candlesticks, pitchers—and decorated quickly with a minimum of concern for line and design. By the turn of the century very little pottery was being made for native use.

Pottery in vogue when the railroads arrived in New Mexico was just as diverse as the pottery of today. Forms and designs varied from area to area but generally not within each one of the pueblos. Uniformity in design schemes and colors within each pueblo seemed to be the rule, although within some villages there was more than one accepted design scheme.

SAN JUAN. Potters of San Juan, and those of nearby Santa Clara, were making burnished black wares in the 1880s. San Juan was also producing burnished red wares. The vessel surfaces were polished but not as diligently as today, and the radiance of the light reflected from the surface was pleasantly muted. In many instances, since less effort was expended in polishing, the surface displayed minute traces left by the polishing stone, which reflected the light unevenly and produced a sheen rather than a gloss to the surface.

One feature of manufacture was common to most San Juan vessels. In applying slip to the vessel the potter covered the upper two-thirds of the surface leaving the lower one-third unslipped. When fired in the usual manner—in an oxidizing atmosphere—the unslipped area was tan and the slipped area was red. When fired to

San Juan burnished black ware (top) and burnished red ware with unslipped tan underbody (bottom), from 1880-1900 period.

15

Two more examples of San Juan burnished red ware with unslipped underbody, 1880-1900 period.

produce a black ware—in a reducing atmosphere—the upper slipped area became a dense black and the lower unslipped area a dark grey with a brown tone.

At San Juan a globular shape for jars was prevalent. This made the vessel height about equal to the diameter and put the widest diameter midway between the rim and the base. The necks were vertical and short. Ornamentation was achieved by varying the profile of the vessel with constricted areas and sometimes with the addition of small loop handles near the rim. Jars which were unornamented sometimes featured a rim which was outcurving.

Some bowls were globular in shape with large orifices formed by incurving body walls, other bowls were shallow with wide-flaring straight sides. However, there were two styles which San Juan potters produced seemingly as a matter of course. One of these forms had the incurving body walls found in the rimless bowls but these popular bowls had a very short outcurving rim rising above the body wall. These bowls were usually red slipped from rim edge down to several inches below the widest diameter, making the bowl a duochrome with red upper-body and tan lower-body.

The other popular bowl form featured a rim which was quite wide and might not be considered a rim at all by some analysts but rather an upper-body. The profile was much the same as most bowls but the upper part (2 to 3 inches wide) was vertical and slightly constricted between the point of juncture with the body wall and the rim edge. This form is a tradition from much earlier days in the pottery making history of the pueblo of San Juan and is known as Kapo Black ware. The constricted vertical upper-body of the later version was red and the lower-body was tan.

Storage jars were very large. These were rarely ornamented in any way. The globular profile was broken only by a very short vertically placed rim.

SANTA CLARA.   Santa Clara was one of the pueblos in which several vessel forms were typical of the ware in the 1870s and 1880s. The globular shape with a short vertical neck, so popular at San Juan, was also made at Santa Clara, but it was not the dominant shape. More popular was a vessel with a tall neck and a body which featured prominent shoulders usually formed by a sharp outward curve at an angle to the base of the neck. The curve of the shoulder stopped very close to the widest diameter and the profile of the body showed a long, almost straight line slanting inward to a small base. The shoulder sometimes displayed a double curve forming a terrace with the lower curve being at the widest diameter, and in other instances the shoulder was formed in the same concept but with ridges taking the place of the curves. The necks of these jars were smooth and undecorated in many cases and in others were ornamented with oblique ridges spiralling upward from the shoulder to the rim, which quite often had a scalloped edge.

Ornamentation of the globular vessels was achieved with indented meanders and other patterns on the upper portion of the vessel body. This globular shape is the one on which the "bear paw" design was later featured.

Another form made at Santa Clara was a large vessel which could perhaps be called a deep bowl. It certainly was not a jar, although it had definite well rounded shoulders similar to those on jars, and the necks were restricted with straight upright walls. Some had slightly outward curving rims. It qualified as a bowl because the diameter was so much greater than the height and the orifice was so very large.

Small bowls for serving food were made in three forms, including ones with incurving vessel walls, vertical walls extending upward

Examples of Santa Clara wares from the 1880-1900 period.

in a curve from a rounded base, and walls which slanted outward with very little curve to terminate in a narrow flat rim.

A double-spouted jar which today is popularly called a "wedding jar" was a form of pottery known to most of the northern New Mexico pottery making groups. This jar shape is also known, in one form or another, in several cultures of the world, both prehistoric and historic. Santa Clara is the one pueblo which made this form famous in northern New Mexico.

SAN ILDEFONSO.   San Ildefonso seems to have been in a transition in pottery decorating in the 1880s. Black abstract geometric designs on a cream colored background were giving way to black and red designs on a cream background. The design concepts didn't change substantially but some design units which had originally been painted black began to appear in red with black outlines. These designs usually were placed in two, or sometimes three, horizontal bands: one or two narrow bands around the neck and shoulder; one wide band covering most of the body. The elements of the designs were quite varied, including angular and curvilinear geometric units, stylized plant forms, and symbolic motifs with the linear and bold, solid elements so well balanced that the whole was an artistic delight.

During the black-on-cream period extremely large storage jars were produced. These storage jars had the same forms as the smaller jars—globular, with a variation in the placement of the widest diameter. Decoration was also the same abstract geometric designs found on the smaller jars. Very large bowls were also produced—some measuring 18 inches in diameter with a 12 inch depth. The walls of these bowls were a continuous outward curve from rounded base to rim.

San Ildefonso black-on-white ware from the 1880-1900 period.

18

Contemporaneous with the black-on-cream design styles was a ware on which the same traditional decorative patterns in black were used but on an all red background. This was a style believed to have its origin just a matter of several decades prior to the 1880s and continued to be made generally only several decades after the 1880s. It was a style produced almost exclusively at San Ildefonso.

The black-on-red wares displayed the same globular shapes as those of the black-on-cream vessels, and with all of the same variations. One feature which seemed to be most popular for vessels of the black-on-red ware was a ridge or ledge on the inner part of the neck about three-fourths of an inch below the rim. It was intended to support a lid, which was convex with a single loop handle at the top of the dome.

Some of the large bowls in the black-on-red ware differed from the black-on-cream in that the last few inches of the upper walls were constricted slightly, giving the rim an outcurving profile. Other large bowls had incurving walls from the widest diameter upward to a rim which was vertical and no higher than one-half inch. Small bowls were generally quite shallow, with outward slanting walls having very little curve. Some of these had a small horizontal projection at the top, placed at right angles to the body wall, forming a flat rim usually about one inch wide.

With the sudden demand for trinkets brought on by the influx of visitors, the black and red (polychrome) wares became increasingly popular with San Ildefonso potters *because* it was more colorful and therefore had more appeal to the tourist. As the polychrome designs gained in favor the vessel form began to change. The black-on-cream wares were predominantly globular in form with an outcurving neck approximately two inches high, more or less, and the widest diameter was sometimes high, giving the jar a

San Ildefonso black-on-white (top two examples) and black-on-red (bottom) from the 1880-1900 period.

19

definite shoulder, sometimes midway between rim and base, accenting the globular form. But beginning to appear was a jar with the widest diameter low on the body, a form which gave the tall neck a certain prominence. It was this last form which became the popular one when polychrome ware superseded the black-on-cream styles. As time advanced this form became standard.

TESUQUE.   In the late 1800s Tesuque women were making pottery vessels which closely resembled those of the neighboring pueblo of San Ildefonso. The forms were similar, the decoration done in black on a cream slip, and the designs were similar except that more linear elements were featured. These are particularly noticeable on the water jars.

Tesuque potters were content to work in the black-on-cream style, never generally developing a polychrome ware as did San Ildefonso potters.

Very large jars, water jars with the several profiles produced at San Ildefonso, and bowls of the shallow form with curved walls, flared walls or straight walls, were all favored at Tesuque. Some wares made at Tesuque and San Ildefonso during the last half of the nineteenth century were so similar that positive identity is sometimes quite difficult.

SANTO DOMINGO.   Late nineteenth century pottery of Santo Domingo Pueblo represented a decorative style which was unlike the styles of other northern New Mexico pueblos. (At San Juan and Santa Clara the wares were solid black and solid red with ornamental features found in the *shape* of the vessel and indentation of the surface. At San Ildefonso, Tesuque, and Cochiti the decoration was ornate and rather intricate and done in black-on-

Tesuque Pueblo pottery from the 1880-1900 era.

cream, with red introduced at San Ildefonso. At Santa Ana, Zia, Laguna, Acoma, and Zuni, located to the south and west of Santo Domingo, the styles featured elaborate polychrome patterns, some bold, some intricate.)

Santo Domingo developed a bold form of ornamentation in black on a cream colored background. It was made up of simple basic geometric elements used in repetition in horizontal bands around the vessel, or in well designed combinations in independent units. Both jars and bowls displayed the two concepts. Jars usually had two horizontal zones, one confined to the neck and the other covering most of the body. Neck zones usually had elements in repetition; the body zones were either basic elements in repetition or the large separate units.

Bowls featured the repetitious treatment on the exterior in most cases (but not exclusively), and on those bowls which were decorated on the interior the large independent motifs were favored and were used as an all over ornamentation, although some had narrow zones of elements in repetition at the rim.

Red was used by Santo Domingo potters as underbody and base slip and in a wide band on the interior of the neck. Red was not often used in the decorative patterns of the early period.

In form, Santo Domingo jars were basically globular but with definite shoulders and constricted necks with flaring rims. The widest diameter was midway between rim and base, or just above midway. Small bowls usually had a simple curve from rim to base with the greatest diameter at the rim. Larger bowls were more varied. Most used the simple forms of the smaller bowls but some had a constricted rim or pronounced flaring rim. Storage jars were predominantly globular with a short, vertical neck and a rounded base.

Three examples of Santo Domingo pottery from the 1880-1900 period.

21

Cochiti Pueblo creations from the 1880-1900 period.

COCHITI. The word was distinctly globular when referring to Cochiti pottery. The jars, the bowls, and the delightful canteen-like vessels were all very round in shape. The spherical form of the water jars and storage jars was broken only by short vertical necks which occasionally had slightly flaring rims. Bowls had incurving walls which extended only a few inches above the widest diameter. The canteen-like vessels were an innovative form which developed at Cochiti. Their round bodies had an opening at the top which was usually spanned by an arched handle. Extending outward from just below the juncture of the handle and the edge of the orifice was a spout which was made in the shape of the head of a bird or animal. These heads were pleasingly molded, although at times abstract and of rather nebulous identity.

Cochiti potters were deft at figure modeling. The art of producing large human figures, caricatures of many non-Indian personages of diverse professions—padre, cowboy, businessman, tourist—which were a popular collector's item in the 1890s, was well known at least a decade earlier. Collected in 1880 was a water jar made in human form.

Cochiti designs done in black on a cream slip were, in part, very much like those of the Santo Domingo geometric patterns and often featured plant forms, animals, birds, and even fish. Symbolic events were occasionally incorporated in both geometric and naturalistic patterns.

Very large bowls decorated on both the exterior and interior were made at Cochiti. The designs on the exterior were bold curvilinear geometric motifs. The distinctive aspect of these bowls was the decoration on the interior. The entire interior was decorated with plant forms which were sometimes abstract and sometimes very realistic. Birds and animals were associated with these plant forms in such a way as to make charming compositions.

SANTA ANA. Carrying on a very long and very strong tradition of vessel form, pottery jars of Santa Ana were consistently globular, with either very short necks or merely vertical extensions of the vessel walls. The orifices were quite wide. Dominant in the designs of black and red on a cream slip were large angular and curvilinear free-form areas of red, which were sometimes outlined with black or partially outlined with black. Complementing these outstanding red areas were small, well designed, intricate elements in black.

The red paint was a rich dark color, the black was thick and intense. The designs were a bold simplification of the patterns seen on the Puname Polychrome wares (A.D. 1700-1800), which were the immediate ancestors of Santa Ana and Zia wares.

The large bowls which were produced at Santa Ana varied somewhat from the ancestral tradition in that the upper walls of the vessels had a strong outward flare instead of the vertical upper walls characteristic of Puname Polychrome. Designs that were used on the jars were also used on the bowls, and were confined to a band placed just below the rim.

ZIA. *Diversity* was expressed at Zia in the decorative schemes rather than in the vessel form. The moderately wide-mouthed jars did not feature a neck, as such, but from the rim the vessel wall slanted outward with a slight incurve for a very short distance before it took a wide smooth outcurve to form the body—and then diminished into another very slight incurve as it met the small base. The widest diameter appeared above the mid-zone of the jars.

Decorative patterns were painted in red-orange and black and appear in three different design schemes. The motif which was identified as being primarily the product of Zia designers featured a wide double meander zone encircling the jar, which swept

Examples of Santa Ana pottery from the 1880-1900 period.

23

Two Zia Pueblo vessels from the 1880-1900 period.

alternately high over the shoulder and low on the body. The supplemental decorative units were geometric, with birds or plant forms used in several combinations.

Some Zia jars had a narrow horizontal decorative zone immediately below the rim with body designs covering the entire area from the decorative zone at the rim to the delineating lines between body and underbody. On other jars not having the decorative rim zone the designs extended from very near the rim over the entire body to the line between the body and underbody.

Large bowls made at Zia were quite deep and the upper few inches of the vessel wall took a definite incurve which put the widest diameter very high on the vessel profile. Designs on these large bowls were, for the most part, geometric and usually featured a wide red angular meander, confined to a horizontal band just below the rim. Small black geometric elements completed the design scheme, enhancing the wide red zones. The walls of small bowls had an outward slant with a short outcurve at the rim. Designs were simple and usually geometric, either angular or curvilinear.

ISLETA.   Isleta potters were the makers of very plain red wares due to the poor quality of the heavy brown clay in their area. Vessels made at this pueblo during the late 1800s take up very little shelf space in the museum or collector's storage area because of their lack of genuine appeal. Isleta pottery was not a "collector's item" from any point of view.

In 1880 a large number of Laguna people moved to a spot very close to Isleta, following a dispute in their own pueblo. They, of course, were the makers of polychrome pottery. Not only did their attractive designs and color schemes catch the eye of the Isleta potter but also the knowledge of using the proper temper to achieve thin walls then became available to the Isleta potter. A few members of the Isleta pottery making community eventually adopted the techniques of making Laguna-type pottery.

LAGUNA.   The design elements displayed on Laguna pottery were those seen on Acoma pottery but the Laguna versions were not as well organized or patterned. Colors used were red, orange, and an orange-yellow outlined and accented with a very dark brown.

Laguna jars were globular with the widest diameter midway between the rim and the base. The slope between the widest diameter and the underbody was a continuous outward curve. Walls of the underbody took an incurve to the base. Necks were usually short and slanted inward to the rim very slightly and without a curve. Some jars displayed a fluted vertical neck and rim.

Most of the bowls took this profile: a continuous outward curve from rim to rounded base with the widest diameter a short distance down from the rim. Designs on bowls were also similar to those of Acoma but much better organized than on the jars. They were polychrome over the entire exterior surface including the base. Another form was also globular with rounded base and wide orifice but had a fluted neck, which was either vertical or slightly out-flaring. Bowls which took this form had a red-slipped base.

Ceramic effigies were collected at Laguna during this period. They were well formed, rounded rather than angular, and decorated with design elements found on jars and bowls. But the identity of the quadruped or bird the potter intended to portray is not easily discernible.

Laguna Pueblo examples of the 1880-1900 period.

25

Two strikingly different Acoma pottery design styles of the 1880-1900 period.

ACOMA.   Designs on water jars made at Acoma Pueblo were well organized in one, or two, and sometimes three horizontal zones, encircling the body from rim to underbody. Acoma potters decorated either with black only or with a combination of black and red.

The white clay found in the Acoma area is an intense white, a pure white, and has been used by Acoma potters for a very long time as a slip for their vessels. This stark white slip and the very thin vessel walls of Acoma pottery were famous even in very early days. Design elements included all of the geometrical units—squares, diamonds, triangles, circles, and crescents—sometimes combined with abstract plant forms and birds.

Water jars had the widest diameter midway between the rim and the base. The outward curve below the widest diameter was slight and diminished to an inward straight slant as it met the base. The neck was formed by a sharp incurving of the vessel wall from the shoulder, and then the wall slanted slightly inward, usually in a straight line, to the rim. Some jars had fluted necks and rims which were vertical or slanted inward to the rim.

Small bowls, in profile, had a continuous curve from rim to base with the widest diameter at the rim. Larger bowls had a similar contour but the widest diameter was several inches below the rim. Bowls were decorated with the same patterns as those on the jars but the designs were applied to a single very wide band encircling the upper body.

ZUNI.   Most Zuni jars had a distinct delineation between the in-sloping neck with small vertical rim and the body of the vessel. Jars had their widest diameter high on the vessel very close to the beginning of the neck slope. The neck made up approximately the upper one-fourth of the vessel. The lower three-fourths of the vessel body was decorated continuously and curved in sharply to a small underbody, which was delineated not only by the lower framing lines of the decorated area but also by color and form. The underbody had a dark brown slip and the wall had a slight out-curve as it joined the very small base.

Designs of Zuni jars of the period were all elaborate and intricate combinations of large and small scrolls, serrated lines, much fine line hachure, deer with the traditional heart-line visible in red, stylized birds, and large circular rosette elements with scalloped perimeters. Design orientation was in both horizontal and vertical panelling.

Bowls were large and comparatively shallow. The walls had three profiles: up-curving from a rounded base to the rim with no undulation; up-curving from a wide flat base with slightly out-slanting rim area; up-curving from a rounded base with a constriction just below the short out-slanting rim. Bowls were decorated on the interior with designs that were seen on the jars, and decorated on the exterior with a serrated diagonal unit featuring several dark triangles on the lower side of a long slanting line and two serrated hook elements which terminated in a dark elongated triangle. The bowl which was not decorated in this manner was a rarity in the period 1880-1900.

Many unusual canteens were made at Zuni at this time. The canteens were varied in form in many ways: globular with short round spouts and two loop handles; barrel-shaped oriented horizontally with rounded enlarged ends, some with ridges; triangular in outline with the orifice at the apex; double-globes, one placed above the other, each with a spout. Designs were the same as those on the jars but not as elaborate or with as many of the design motifs used together.

Richly decorated Zuni wares of the 1880-1900 period.

Another pottery style made at Zuni, about which very little is known yet which was contemporaneous with the polychrome styles of this period, was one that featured linear geometric designs painted white on a red background. The designs were typical of Zuni at this time but were in outline only, and the form of the vessel was traditional as well. Since very few of these vessels are in collections, public or private, it can be assumed that not many were made.

At Zuni the owl figurine was a favorite. Late in the nineteenth century these owls were molded and painted in a very realistic manner.

A Zuni Pueblo example from the 1880-1900 era.

28

2 · REVITALIZATION OF A FINE CRAFT

Although the invasion of northern New Mexico by non-Indian individuals had adverse effects on the Indian way of life and disrupted a centuries-long tradition of pottery making, this influx of strangers—with their centuries-long tradition for getting things organized—was not all bad.

The newcomers recognized the great worth of Indian ability, and through some of their societies, institutions of learning, and activities, sought an understanding of the Indian and his ways.

This led to an awareness on the part of the strangers of the Indian need for financial stability and they set out to find a way to give assistance.

1880: ESTABLISHMENT OF THE HISTORICAL SOCIETY OF NEW MEXICO

The Historical Society of New Mexico was actually organized December 26, 1859, but adjourned *sine die* September 23, 1863. Then on December 27, 1880 the organization was re-established. With the Hon. William G. Rich, the Hon. L. Bradford Prince, David J. Miller, William M. Berger and Lehman Spiegelberg listed as officers, an annual appropriation (begun in 1882) from the Territory of New Mexico, and with the use of several rooms in the Palace of the Governors (then Federally owned and set aside for the Society's use in 1885), the Historical Society of New Mexico began anew its stated task of preserving history.

This renewal of the Historical Society had no immediate influence on pottery making or pottery styles, but because Historical Society collections included Indian pottery, the activities of this organization had a profound effect on Pueblo pottery of a later day. The members of the Society had an opportunity to collect pottery which was totally native, totally uninfluenced by Anglo contact, and they took advantage of that opportunity.

The collection of late nineteenth century pottery which the Historical Society assembled was eventually put into the custody of the Museum of New Mexico and became a part of the research and exhibit resources from which Pueblo potters still receive inspiration. Beginners and experienced potters visit the pottery storage areas in the Laboratory of Anthropology in Santa Fe to study the "old" designs—designs which are a part of their heritage but not a part of their every day lives because only in museums and private collections are these treasures preserved.

1907: ARCHAEOLOGICAL EXCAVATIONS ON THE PAJARITO PLATEAU

Archaeological excavations on the Pajarito Plateau were begun in 1907 by Dr. Edgar L. Hewett, Director of the School of American Archaeology, later to be known as the School of American Research. San Ildefonso men were employed to do the digging. The men discussed the daily activities with their wives and sometimes brought home potsherds to show to them. The women became very interested in the pottery which was coming out of the

San Ildefonso pottery (opposite page and above) of the 1900-1920 period.

31

Pottery from Santa Clara Pueblo made during the 1900-1920 period.

"dig" and some of them began to make pottery again. Dr. Hewett and Kenneth M. Chapman (then a member of Dr. Hewett's field crew as artist), encouraged the women to make good traditional pottery. This they did, but progress was slow because there was not then a market for this type of pottery. The tourists continued to prefer water pitchers, candle holders, rain gods, and other knick-knacks.

However, the potters continued to respond to the encouragement they received and in a few years skills had developed to the degree that Antonita (Tonita) Roybal, Ramona Gonzales, Maximiliana Martinez, and Maria Martinez were making fine vessels. By 1915 Maria had attained a skill that surpassed the others. During these years Maria made polychrome first and then the black-on-red wares. Polished black ware was also re-introduced.

1909: FOUNDING OF THE MUSEUM OF NEW MEXICO

In 1906 the Archaeological Institute of America had been incorporated by the U.S. Congress; in the following year the Institute made a proposition to the Territory of New Mexico to locate its School of American Archaeology in Santa Fe. It was through Dr. Edgar L. Hewett, spokesman for the School, that the request was made. As it worked out, the School of American Archaeology (reorganized in 1917 as the School of American Research) would manage the Museum of New Mexico, which would be housed in the Palace of the Governors, and Dr. Hewett would act as the director of the two organizations.

The Territorial Legislature of 1909 created the Museum of New Mexico and gave custodianship of the Palace of the Governors to

PUEBLO POTTERY'S MANY SHAPES AND COLORS. Inventiveness of San Ildefonso potters during the first two decades of this century is evident in the examples at left and right. Polychrome water jar (right center) is typical of Zia wares of early 1900s. Polished black wedding jar from Santa Clara (left center) was produced during pottery's design revival. (Height of vessels, from left: 3½″, 13″, 9¾″, 6¾″.)

LEFT: San Ildefonso produced two quite different styles during 1900-1920 period. Polychrome jar at left was made by Maria and decorated by Julian Martinez (13¼″ dia.). Red jar on the right, maker unknown, is typical of the black-on-red wares of the era.

OPPOSITE PAGE, LEFT: Storage jar decorated by Julian Martinez at peak of his stylized-geometric period (18″ dia.). UPPER RIGHT: Acoma jar of early 1900s shows the ability of some unknown designer to adapt a square pattern to curved surface (12¼″ dia.). LOWER RIGHT: Superb sense of order, balance, and complexity within simplicity is evident in the design of this water jar of Zuni from the early 1920s (14″ dia.).

MODERN MINIATURES. From left: Tiny jars with punched design, made by Myra Little Snow, Santa Clara, 1976 (2″ and 1½″ high). Jar highlighted with inset of turquoise by TsePe and Dora, San Ildefonso, 1974 (3½″). Widemouth jar with punched design by Myra Little Snow, 1976 (2½″). Undecorated jar by Irene TsePe, 1976 (2¼″). Closed bowl with carved design by Lucy Year Flower, Pojoaque, 1974 (2″).

PUEBLO POTTERY'S PRACTICALITY. This well designed Santo Domingo bowl was produced in the early 1930s probably to attract a buyer, yet like much Pueblo pottery it is useful as well as decorative, as demonstrated here by the colorful Indian corn it holds (9¼″ dia.).

BIRDS OF ACOMA (ABOVE): Birds were a popular design motif at Acoma in the early 1900s. The two large jars are typical of this early work (both ca. 13″ dia.). Smaller one at center shows a later concept of the popular motif (6½″ dia.).

MODERN FIGURINES FROM COCHITI (LEFT): Cochiti potters have long been famous for their intriguing figurines. Storyteller at left was made in 1975 by Aurelia Suina (8″ high). Bread-lady was created in 1960 by Teresita Romero (7″ high).

BIRDS OF ZIA (OPPOSITE PAGE): Birds were nearly as important a theme at Zia as they were at Acoma. Example at right is from early 1900s (11¾″ dia.). Smaller jar at center was probably produced in the 1930s (5½″ dia.). Jar at left met the challenge of new style development and won prize for its maker, Lociana Shije, in 1941 (16″ dia.).

FANCIFUL DESIGN FROM COCHITI. Stephani Herrera, an imaginative potter from Cochiti Pueblo, combined the figurine motif and the traditional water jar shape and design in this delightful creation from the 1950s (7″ dia.).

the School of American Archaeology. Before the end of the next decade the personnel of the Museum of New Mexico had become very much involved in the ever-changing picture of Pueblo pottery making.

1917: EFFORTS TO IMPROVE POTTERY

A project which had its beginnings in 1917, and lasted but three years, had the beneficial effect on pottery making which was originally intended, but that result came about later and in an unforeseen manner.

Mme. Vera von Blumenthal of Russia and Miss Rose Dougan of Richmond, Indiana, arrived in northern New Mexico in 1917 to work with potters of San Ildefonso to help improve the quality of their ceramics. The length of time they were able to devote to this project with the potters was limited to several months during the summer seasons, and by the end of the summer of 1919 it was obvious that very little had been accomplished. The two ladies offered to turn their project over to Dr. Edgar L. Hewett, Director of the Museum of New Mexico, and to provide $200 for a year's supervision of the project. Dr. Hewett accepted the offer. Kenneth Chapman and Wesley Bradfield, employees of the Museum, were appointed to carry out the details.

In the next several years these two had demonstrated to the potters through the practical application of sales at higher prices for top quality pottery that their efforts, though more time consuming, were well worth that extra time spent. Maria and Julian Martinez benefitted almost immediately and Tonita Roybal very soon afterward.

And so the stage was set for the big event of 1922—The Southwest Indian Fair.

Examples produced from about 1917 to the time of the First Annual Southwest Indian Fair in 1922: Santa Clara (top), and San Ildefonso (bottom).

33

Tesuque pottery (top two examples) and a Santo Domingo vessel (bottom) made from about 1917 to the time of the First Annual Southwest Indian Fair in 1922.

1919: REVIVAL OF FIESTA DE SANTA FE

After World War I, when it was possible to resume a normal way of life once more, the Santa Fe Fiesta was revived. Indian participation was featured in these revived celebrations and pageantry. Indian governors took part in the opening ceremonies, Indians were included in the cast of the De Vargas Reconquest pageant, and Indian dances enlivened the activities of all four days of the celebration.

It was also reported by Paul A. F. Walter in *Art and Archaeology* (Vol. IX, No. 1) that "Under the Palace portals sat Indian vendors of pottery and beadwork."

1922: FIRST ANNUAL SOUTHWEST INDIAN FAIR

During the Fiesta of 1922 the Indians had the privilege of taking on a new role in the annual celebration. An Indian Fair, the first to be held in Santa Fe, was to be part of the Fiesta. The Fair was announced in the July issue of EL PALACIO of that year, over the signature of Dr. E. L. Hewett, Director of the Museum of New Mexico and School of American Research:

The First Annual Southwest Indian Fair and Industrial Arts and Crafts Exhibition, limited strictly to Indian entry and competition, and participated in by the various tribes and pueblos of the southwest, is the first of its character ever held in this section. Local Indian fairs have been held on reservations and at some of the county fairs in New Mexico there have been exhibits of Indian handiwork, but nothing of the scope and character of the exhibition herein contemplated has ever been witnessed in New Mexico or Arizona.

34

The objects of the exhibition are encouragement of native arts and crafts among the Indians; to revive old arts; to keep the arts of each tribe and pueblo as distinct as possible; the establishment and locating of markets for all Indian products; the securing of reasonable prices; authenticity of all handicrafts offered for sale and protection to the Indian in all his business dealing with traders and buyers.

The exhibition is the outgrowth of ideas advanced several years ago by Miss Rose Dougan of Richmond, Indiana, who has interested herself in a practical way in Indian handicrafts and has tendered an endowment from the income of which some of the prizes herein offered are in part derived.

The business interests of Santa Fe and some of our citizens, non-residents of the capital, sensing the great value to the Indians, state and nation, of this enterprise, have been liberal in their responses to requests for trophies and prizes.

The Bureau of Indian Affairs has tendered and is giving its cordial co-operation in making the exhibition a success.

It is not expected that the initial effort will be productive of anything spectacular, either in quality or dimension, but it is sincerely hoped and believed that the beginning thus made will result in future exhibitions of the greatest industrial and economic value to all classes of citizens, particularly to the Indian.

All prizes and trophies will be paid and delivered immediately following the making of awards.

A competent jury of awards, consisting of three members, will be appointed by the Director of the School of American Research.

Mr. Lansing B. Bloom, Assistant Director of the State Museum, will have charge of all exhibits and has been appointed superintendent of exhibits. All exhibits must be

Bowls made during the era of the first Indian Fairs of the 1920s: Cochiti (top two), and Santo Domingo (bottom) examples.

35

San Ildefonso pot (top) typical of those which were quickly being taken from the region prior to the 1920s. Santa Ana jar (center) and Tesuque jar (bottom) from era of first Indian Fairs.

delivered to him at the state armory, Santa Fe, not later than Saturday, September 2, 1922.

SCHOOL OF AMERICAN RESEARCH
EDGAR L. HEWETT, *Director*

SANTA FE CHAMBER OF COMMERCE
R. E. TWITCHELL, *President*
WALTER M. DANBURG, *Secretary*

The State Armory in which this first "Fair and Exhibition" was held is today the Museum of New Mexico's Hall of the Southwest Indian, located to the rear of the Palace of the Governors. Attractive premium lists were available. The fair, of course, provided prizes for *all* the crafts, but in designing the premium list and the official souvenir program for the first Annual Southwest Indian Fair the chairmen of the festivities obviously had pottery on their minds. Pueblo pottery designs—clouds and lightning symbols and a San Ildefonso bird—were printed in the polychrome pottery colors of black and red on earth brown.

THE DOUGAN FUND PRIZES

The prizes provided by the Rose Dougan Fund were fairly generous ($5.00 First Prize, $2.00 Second Prize) considering that it was 1922 when a dollar bought so much more than it does today. First and second prizes were offered for the "best exhibit of pottery, not more than three specimens, by an individual exhibitor" from each of the following pueblos:

San Juan	San Felipe	Isleta
Santa Clara	Santa Ana	Laguna
San Ildefonso	Zia	Acoma
Tesuque	Jemez	Zuni
Santo Domingo	Sandia	Hopi
Cochiti		

This system of awarding prizes stimulated competition between individual potters of each village, which was one of the objectives toward which Miss Dougan had been working. In addition, there were special prizes for large jars, decorated and undecorated, over 50 inches in diameter; for a new type of decorated pottery; and, as stated in the premium list, a "grand prize for the best exhibit, not more than three specimens, by an individual exhibitor, from any of the foregoing Pueblos." Here was competition between individual potters of the entire Pueblo region.

Sixteen pueblos were listed. In EL PALACIO, October 16, 1922, we find the names of the potters who were awarded the prizes at the First Annual Southwest Indian Fair. These potters represented nine of the pueblos:

San Juan	Tesuque	Zia
Santa Clara	Santo Domingo	Isleta
San Ildefonso	Cochiti	Acoma

Since prizes were offered for the "best" of each pueblo, it could probably be safely assumed that the nine villages represented were the only ones which entered pottery, and undoubtedly were the only ones in which pottery was produced in quantities large enough to interest potters in the exhibition, competition, and market opportunities. Documentation and museum collections tend to give proof to this assumption.

Pueblo pottery of this type was rapidly being taken from the Southwest prior to the 1920s. Examples from Acoma (top) and Zia Pueblos.

The awards made in 1923 at the second Fair went to representatives of the same nine pueblos. However, there was a change in the names of the prize winners, indicating that the competition was effective.

In 1924 Jemez Pueblo entered pottery in the Fair for the first time. It was reported that this was the first pottery made in 150 years at the pueblo.

In 1926 pottery made at Zuni was entered in the Fair for the first time.

1900-1920: CHANGES IN POTTERY FORMS AND DESIGNS

Pottery made during the first two decades of the twentieth century underwent minor changes in some pueblos, major changes in other pueblos. These changes are recorded in documents and in museum collections, both positively and negatively. The written word is scattered through many publications, a bit here, a bit there.

Several museum collections were being formed at the time but had not reached the stage of explicit record keeping, and dating of pottery specimens was rare. However, knowledge of this period in pottery making is available, some of it quite specific.

SAN JUAN.   At San Juan the quality and quantity of pottery decreased. Some traditional wares were made but small novelties were featured towards the end of this period.

SANTA CLARA.   Traditional Santa Clara polished black wares were continued in decreasing quantity. However, those that were produced were expertly made with well-proportioned traditional forms. Undoubtedly these were made by the experienced potters, older potters who kept to the older ways.

The novelty wares, small and in non-traditional forms, were being made in ever increasing numbers. Small jars, candlesticks, moccasins in clay, and *animalitos* were to be seen everywhere, readily available for the next tourist.

Santa Clara vessels (top), and an elaborately decorated jar from San Ildefonso, from the 1900-1920 period.

SAN ILDEFONSO.   It was in 1919 that Julian Martinez developed the technique for producing a design scheme featuring the combination of polished black and matte black on pottery surfaces. At that early date in the development of the new style there was much that needed doing to bring the ware to its ultimate perfection. Once started it didn't take long to produce the superb designing that has made this ware famous around the world, since Maria's jars and bowls were at that time recognized for their well-proportioned profiles.

During this period the polychrome wares that had become popular before the turn of the century had reached a point where the red introduced as an accent became featured in well-designed decorative patterns, and a good balance between black and red was achieved on a vessel which had its widest diameter very low on the body. The upperbody and neck made up two-thirds of a vessel which had a gracefully sweeping inward curve from the widest diameter upward to an outcurving rim. It was on this upper area that the bold curvilinear black and red designs appeared.

The black and red style so popular in the late 1880s declined in popularity and by 1920 only one pottery making family continued to produce this attractive ware.

TESUQUE.   Tesuque, too, was searching for new ideas. Some of the potters who continued to make pottery in the traditional manner experimented with variations in form and color, but many of the potters went the road of novelties, the "curios" that *looked Indian* and sold quickly in great volume. It was said of this era that if the white man would buy it, the Indian would make it—and it is very hard to argue with a steady income.

"Raingods" were in vogue and were being exploited by many of the traders, particularly John S. Candelario of the Original Curio Store in Santa Fe. Experiments of all kinds were being made but one experiment which was one of a kind even at Tesuque resulted in small shallow bowls and other knickknacks with a light beige slip and linear designs in red, green and blue—designs which were rather indistinct. The use of water colors or diluted colored ink on these little objects is suspected.

SANTO DOMINGO.   Production of the traditional Santo Domingo geometric designs on traditional Santo Domingo shapes continued into the early 1900s on a diminished scale, but something new was added in this period. A potter by the name of Mrs. Ramon Garcia created a unique style which could have been called "negative boldface" if one were inclined to invent pottery type names. The typical Santo Domingo angular geometric design elements in repetition on typical early Santo Domingo forms were featured. These she painted black on a cream slip in the traditional way, but areas left unpainted or "open" in the traditional designs were painted red or sometimes black in this distinctive style. The two painted areas were separated by a very narrow straight unpainted area which, when well done, became a framing line for the painted areas. Most of the known jars of this style appear to have been made by Mrs. Garcia and were produced in the early 1900s. Her death was recorded in 1915. If the style was carried on by other potters it was not for long.

COCHITI.   Cochiti potters continued to make household pottery vessels, storage jars, and large and small bowls in the traditional forms and designs. They preferred Pueblo-made vessels to the commercially produced enamelware, china and so forth, although

Tesuque figurine and curio ware from the 1900-1920 era (top), and two Santo Domingo jars (bottom) from the same period.

41

Cochiti Pueblo creations from the 1900-1920 period.

they usually traded with Zia, Acoma and Zuni for the thin walled water jars which Cochiti householders considered to be superior to their own jars.

Those potters who excelled in the making of figurines, particularly animals, always had a good market for their handwork, so there was no decline in the production of this ware.

Pottery making was never quite as vital at Cochiti as a source of income as it was at some of the other pueblos, partially because of the well-known quality of the Cochiti drums, for which there was always a good market. The production volume of sale pottery was not large at this time because geographically Cochiti was not on the tourist trail as yet. Objects made for sale were marketed through the traders in Santa Fe, Bernalillo, and probably Albuquerque.

Santa Ana.   The decline in pottery making was quite sharp at Santa Ana following the turn of the century. Pottery that was produced was not well made, designs were less imaginative and not as well executed.

Zia.   Forms and designs of the late nineteenth century were continued into the twentieth century. The bold overall geometric patterns, the birds, the plants, the double red meander sweeping upward and downward around the jars were still featured with very few changes. There were, of course, minor changes as time went by because the older potters no longer worked at the ceramic arts, and younger potters, with new ideas, began their careers in clay.

Isleta.   Documentation on Isleta pottery for this period is as rare as the pottery itself, but presumably the traditional red wares and the newly adopted Laguna-type polychrome wares were being made in a fair quantity.

LAGUNA.   Acoma and Laguna wares of this period were quite similar. The design patterns were intricate combinations of angular and curvilinear geometrical elements, fine line hachure, and plant forms (stylized leaves and flowers) with much more color than on earlier vessels. These two pueblos had begun to feature red, muted orange, yellow-orange with accents, and outlines of dark brown in their designs and were the only New Mexico pueblos which would regularly use more than one color in their decorative schemes.

By this time the jar forms were a little less globular, having taller necks with more vertical walls, and the widest diameter was above the mid-point between the rim and base. Jar shoulders were more pronounced.

In 1910 Miss Josephine Ford, an eastern potter who later settled in Colorado, built a kiln at Laguna, after trying to introduce glazing at Acoma with no success. Her objective was to produce glazed and unglazed tiles, kiln fired, for sale in the eastern markets. A few Laguna potters participated in this project. Volkmer glazes were used but these negated the black and red native Laguna pigments so special commercial pigments were employed when the tiles were to be glazed. If Miss Ford's sole intent was to establish at Laguna a flourishing business in Southwestern Indian-made tiles for eastern sales her efforts were unsuccessful.

ACOMA.   With the progression of time changes are inevitable even in a pottery style which is quite stable. This was true of Acoma pottery wares. Continued were the overall bold geometric patterns, either in several horizontal zones from rim to underbody or in a pattern without zones. These geometric patterns were accented with curvilinear elements, stylized plant forms and fine line diamonds, triangles, and bordering units.

A change which was most evident during this time was the use of

A typical Laguna jar (top) and two examples from Acoma, of the 1900-1920 period.

43

a yellow-orange paint in combination with the red paint. Large geometric areas in yellow-orange and large geometric areas in red, adjoined or opposed, were usually the featured motif. The two colors were also used in well designed patterns of birds complimented by elaborate plant forms—flowers, leaves, seedpods. In some decorative schemes a muted orange paint was also seen. Vessel forms of the late nineteenth century remained stable with only variations employed by the individual makers.

ZUNI.   A decline in pottery making at Zuni during the early 1900s was beginning to be quite evident. Traditional forms and designs were continued but the production of those wares diminished in favor of jewelry making. Silversmithing had proved to be far more remunerative than pottery making, and those potters who were capable of mastering silversmithing or lapidary techniques abandoned the ceramic arts.

Zuni jars (above) and typical owl figurine from the 1900-1920 period.

Awareness of Indian heritage and of Indian potential of the moment and for the future was rather widespread during the year of the first annual Indian Fair. Three organizations dedicated to the several aspects of Indian life came into being.

Those individuals within these organizations who had set out to find a way to help the Indian realize his potential had found it in pottery. They began an extensive program to create an appreciation of Indian art by both Indians and non-Indians.

The program moved slowly but positively over a period of years and was completely successful eventually.

1922: BEGINNINGS OF THE INDIAN ARTS FUND

The event that led to the founding of the Indian Arts Fund is legendary—knowledge of it is perpetuated not by the written word but by the spoken word. The legend tells of a very small dinner party at the home of a Tesuque, N.M., resident. Just prior to the arrival of the guests a pottery jar from Zuni Pueblo had been broken, and the pieces placed on the front porch for further disposal. They were seen by the guests as each entered the house.

Discussion during that evening centered on the regrettable loss of beautiful pottery made by the Pueblo Indians either through breakage or by being transported to the far corners of the world by collectors or curio hunters. It was agreed that something should be done about this deplorable situation. And they did it. They interested two individuals who worked with Indian pottery professionally and a medical doctor whose very strong interest in Indian pottery was then but a hobby.

These three, Kenneth M. Chapman and Wesley Bradfield, of the Museum of New Mexico, and Dr. Harry P. Mera, who became a leading archaeologist associated with the Laboratory of Anthropology (which was still a part of the future), along with the hostess of the dinner party, Elizabeth S. Sergent, a writer, organized what they called the "Pueblo Pottery Fund." The broken jar was mended and was cataloged as *Number 1* in the collection they intended to make.

A number of years later Dr. Mera related that they intended to assemble a representative collection of perhaps fourteen or fifteen pieces of pottery from each pueblo, then conclude the project. Three years and over four hundred pots later these four addicted people realized that they had just begun their project.

On November 6, 1925, the Indian Arts Fund came into being, legally incorporated under the New Mexico law, dedicated to collecting, preserving, and studying all Indian art. These activities, which started with the Pueblo Pottery Fund of 1922, continued vigorously for fifty years. In 1972 the group felt that their work was done at last and disbanded. The price of Indian art had so escalated that the "fund" could no longer keep pace.

As it was with the founding of the Historical Society so it was with the organization of the Indians Arts Fund. The impact of the "event" in 1922 on the development of pottery form and design was not felt immediately. The impact came years later when the Indians became aware of their great heritage and sought it in the museum where the pottery has been so carefully preserved.

Fine examples of Acoma pottery (opposite page and above) which were collected by New Mexico organizations in the early 1920s to prevent them from being taken out of the region.

1922:   THE SOUTHWESTERN ASSOCIATION ON INDIAN AFFAIRS

The founding of the New Mexico Association on Indian Affairs (later to be known as the Southwestern Association on Indian Affairs) didn't have a direct effect on the quality of Pueblo pottery for a number of years after its organization but its impact on the quality of Pueblo lives was made immediately.

A number of concerned Santa Feans banded together to protest the passage of the Bursum Bill by the U.S. Congress. The bill would have confirmed to non-Indian residents the land they occupied within the pueblo land grants in New Mexico, and would have favored those non-Indians in the all-important matter of water rights. The bill was defeated. Francis C. Wilson, the attorney representing the NMAIA in the protest, suggested an alternative measure to Senator Bursum, which provided for creation of the Public Lands Board, the function of which was to determine the validity of claims to Indian land.

The goal of the NMAIA, as stated in its first annual report, was "to forward legislation providing an equitable adjustment of land questions between Indians and non-Indians." With the creation of the Public Lands Board this goal was reached. However, just as the Indian Arts Fund realized that its work was not completed when its original objective had been achieved, so too did the NMAIA find that their aims had to be expanded. Legal rights, welfare matters, health, and higher education were eventually to become of great concern to the organization.

In 1933 it merged with the Southwest Indian Fair Committee to continue the encouragement of authentic arts and crafts. Under the supervision of the NMAIA the concept of "fair" was quite

Two fine Zia vessels, among the wares which were collected by New Mexico groups in the early 1920s to prevent native pottery from being taken out of the Southwest.

successfully changed to the concept of "market." Other activities were a part of the program launched by the NMAIA: exhibits were arranged, lectures by experts were held to inform the buying public about traditional Indian products, articles on various aspects of Indian arts, crafts and lifeways were published in New Mexico Magazine. So, the Indian Market that we witness in August of every year had begun its fantastic growth and benefit to the artists and craftsmen of the southwestern Indian world.

In addition to the Indian Market, which is a monumental task, the SWAIA (as stated in its quarterly publication) continues to be "dedicated to helping the Indian people of the Southwest safeguard their rights, preserve their customs and be secure in their own way of life."

1922: BEGINNINGS OF THE INTER-TRIBAL INDIAN CEREMONIAL

On the last weekend of September, 1922, the first Inter-Tribal Indian Ceremonial was held just outside the small southwestern town of Gallup, New Mexico. Envisaged by a group of farsighted civic leaders, the Ceremonial through the years has introduced to hundreds of thousands of interested and curious people the wonder of many tangible and visible aspects of Indian life.

The spectators came by railroad or in the few automobiles then in the southwest, over rough, unpaved roads, to the town of Gallup, population then about 4,000.

Horace Moses (who for many years was a well known public figure in New Mexico) was the driving force and president during the first sixteen years of the Ceremonial. Glenn Emmons, who later became Commissioner of Indian Affairs (1953-1961), served on the Board of the Ceremonial during its first two decades.

Jars from Tesuque (top), Santo Domingo (center), and San Ildefonso (bottom), produced in the 1920-1940 period.

In the early years, financial support of the Ceremonial was far from overwhelming, but in 1939 the event was singled out by the legislature as the state's outstanding tourist attraction and given status of an official state agency with an annual appropriation from state funds.

The Ceremonial was not founded with the same concepts as the Southwestern Indian Fair and has never operated in the same manner. Pictures of the old exhibit hall show many Navajo blankets hanging from the ceiling, exhibited on the walls, and draped over the counters. Since the Ceremonial depended on reservation traders and Indian agencies for its displays, Navajo rugs dominated the colorful interior of the large hall. Traders and collectors were encouraged to exhibit Indian craft-arts and competition between individual craftsmen and artists did not come until later.

The Ceremonial's impact on pottery making therefore was not felt at once, but it was felt eventually, just as it was in the case of the other organizations founded in the same year. Today the Ceremonial and the Indian Market in Santa Fe are equally important to the potter and most of the potters exhibit and compete for prizes at both of these world famous events.

A REVIVAL OF POTTERY MAKING

By the early 1920s the monetary need of Pueblo families had increased because their way of life had changed, and the decline in rainfall continued to make crops less and less dependable. Thus an alternative to the "old way" was very desirable.

Between 1900 and 1920 efforts to improve the quality of San Ildefonso pottery had been moderately successful. Several potters

were producing wares which were of good traditional form and design, and the wisdom of offering these quality wares for sale had been demonstrated with an increase in income. The Indian realized that this could be one of the means to a better way of life.

Following the Indian Fair of 1922 those who had encouraged the San Ildefonso potters to revive "good" pottery began to expand their encouragement to the rest of the Pueblo world. Slowly a true revival of pottery making did take place.

During this revival of pottery making for the retail trade there was a wide search for *new ideas*—much experimentation took place, and attempts to create eye-catching wares were made by most of the imaginative potters. Some of the results were good, some were not, but many were the forerunners of today's well-established design systems.

1923-1928: CHAPMAN AND HALSETH BRING INSPIRATION

Kenneth M. Chapman, a commercial artist, became interested in Pueblo pottery very soon after his arrival in New Mexico in 1899. He was employed at the Las Vegas Normal School (now Highlands University) as art instructor. Dr. Edgar L. Hewett was the president of the Normal School, and so began a professional relationship that lasted many years, concentrated for the most part on Indian pottery.

With the establishment of the Museum of New Mexico in Santa Fe in 1909, Chapman became one of the first members of Director Hewett's staff. He was the artist of Hewett's field crew in the Frijoles and Chaco Canyon excavations.

Zuni jar from the 1920-1940 era (opposite page), and Santo Domingo examples of pottery design that resulted from efforts to encourage a revival in good form and design (above).

51

Examples of pottery design from Zia which resulted from efforts to encourage a revival of quality form and design among Pueblo potters (above and opposite page).

His interest in pottery increased. He began making photographs and drawings of pottery designs and his life's work took shape. The drawings and photographs, while awaiting their ultimate assignment as illustrative material for his many published works, were put to very good use as reference material for the Indian potters themselves during the revival of their craft.

During the days of the Rito de los Frijoles excavations pot sherds dug up were accurately drawn and identified and then made available to the potters of San Ildefonso.

In 1923, Odd S. Halseth, a Veterans Bureau student assigned to the School of American Research for three years intensive museum training, armed himself with Kenneth Chapman's photographs of old Zia pottery and spent several months at the pueblo of Zia, working with the potters there and encouraging them to use and improve on the heritage of their own native designs. The "borrowed" Acoma and Zuni decorative schemes were abandoned and distinctive Zia patterns adopted.

The native Zia pottery designs were indeed distinctive and the traders in the immediate Zia area began to take notice. Both potters and traders benefitted.

In 1924 Halseth visited Jemez, where no pure Jemez-made pottery had been produced in the past hundred years. What pottery was produced at Jemez had been made by potters from other pueblos who had married into that pueblo. Halseth had also brought photos and drawings of old Jemez designs secured from sherds of early excavations in the Jemez area. To attest to the success of his venture, pottery from Jemez was exhibited at the 1925 Indian Fair.

Because of the proximity of Santo Domingo Pueblo the main north-south New Mexico highway this pueblo was producing more "junk" for roadside sales than any other pueblo. Halseth visited the potters of Santo Domingo with hopes of changing their ways but his project was not accepted. The Pueblo Elders did not want the Santo Domingo women to take pottery to the Indian Fair. The consistent Santo Domingo annual winner of first prizes at the Fair, Monica Silva, an excellent potter, was not Santo Domingo born; her pottery was not always typical Santo Domingo pottery, and her attitudes were not those of Santo Domingo. The second prize winners in the years of 1924 and 1926, Tonita Quintana and Felipa Aguilar, had defied the wishes of the pueblo officials—for reasons we will never know.

The New Mexico Association on Indian Affairs, concerned always with the welfare of the Indians, was active in the work of helping the potters raise the quality of their wares. In 1927, at the July executive committee meeting of the Indian Arts Fund, a spokesman for the Association asked the Indian Arts Fund to prepare material to be placed in Pueblo Day Schools for the purpose of encouraging Indian children to appreciate and study their own art.

The request soon became reality. Chapman made available twenty photographs for the Association to use in the schools. The Indian Arts Fund also authorized him to prepare drawings of the elements of Cochiti pottery designs for use in Pueblo schools. A year later, a collection of his photographs of pottery, expertly tinted, were prepared for use in the schools at Cochiti and Zuni.

1931: THE EXPOSITION OF INDIAN TRIBAL ARTS

In *Introduction to American Indian Art,* the booklet issued as part of this exposition, the goals of the event were defined:

Two fine examples of traditional pottery forms (from Acoma) which influenced the pottery produced in New Mexico's pueblos in the 1930s.

The Exposition of Indian Tribal Arts, Inc. was organized in 1930 for the purpose of stimulating and supporting American Indian artists by creating a wider interest and more intelligent appreciation of their work in the American public at large, and to demonstrate to the country what important contribution to our culture the Indian is making. To this end, an exhibition of Indian products in the fine arts and applied arts, selected from the best material available, both old and new, has been arranged.

Although the various organizations in Santa Fe which were interested in promoting Indian art (including the New Mexico Association on Indian Affairs, the Indian Arts Fund, and the Museum of New Mexico) were not officially the sponsors of this exposition, many of their numbers, acting individually, were very much a part of its success. John Sloan, the artist, was president of the corporation; Miss Amelia E. White was chairman of the Executive Committee; and members of the Board of Directors were Santa Feans Margretta S. Dietrich, Oliver La Farge, and Martha White. Those who loaned exhibit material also included many members of the Santa Fe community.

One feature of the Exposition was that Indian material was available for sale to those interested in acquiring Indian art. The Indian material from New Mexico was selected at the 1931 Southwest Indian Fair. That year the Indian Fair Committee bought the best of the wares brought to the Fair, with the specific purpose of sending it to the Exposition.

In a letter from the Indian Fair Committee to the governors of the pueblos, dated June 6, 1931, it was stated: "Next winter in New York there will be an exhibition of Indian Art from all over the

United States. We will send the exhibit from here to New York so that the New Mexico Indians will have their part in the exhibit in New York . . . so that the people in New York will know what beautiful things are made in New Mexico."

1931: OPENING OF THE LABORATORY OF ANTHROPOLOGY

Founded in 1927 as a research organization, the Laboratory of Anthropology opened to the public in December, 1931. The Indian Arts Fund collection was housed in the new building and remained there for many years. Kenneth Chapman and Dr. Harry Mera of Indian Arts Fund fame were members of the new organization, and during the years that followed they continued to pursue their interest in collecting, preserving and studying all Indian art.

The Laboratory's aims were the same as those of the Indian Arts Fund—and archaeology was added thus giving a new dimension by combining the old with the new. In 1947 the Laboratory became a division of the Museum of New Mexico. The anthropological collections in the custody of the Museum were moved to the "Lab" and the collecting, preserving, studying went right on and continues today.

The collections, the knowledge of the staff and research facilities are all available to serious researchers, artists and writers. Indian potters have studied the pottery collections and used the research facilities for many years—the result being innovation as well as an upgrading of the quality of pottery form and design based on the "old" traditional wares produced at pueblos in the past.

Traditional pottery form examples from Zia Pueblo, typical of those which influenced the pottery made in the 1930s at New Mexico pueblos.

Examples of traditional pottery forms from Santa Clara (top), and Acoma (bottom), which influenced pottery produced during the 1930s.

1932: INDIAN SCHOOL PRIZE-WINNERS

At the request of the U.S. Indian Service, Kenneth Chapman served as Supervisor of Indian Arts and Crafts for Indian schools during his first years at the Laboratory of Anthropology. His photographs and drawings of Indian designs served well in this program. This was clearly shown at the Inter-Tribal Indian Ceremonial at Gallup, in 1932, where the exhibit of the Santa Fe Indian School, consisting almost entirely of arts and crafts, won thirty-two blue ribbons and the Grand prize. It is regrettable that the names of the students exhibiting at the Ceremonial are not available because Chapman related at the time that several "future, well known potters" were in the making.

1933-1934: PWAP AND WPA

During the Great Depression the Public Works of Art Project and the Works Progress Administration commissioned many artists to produce works of art for display in public buildings being constructed at that time. Several Pueblo potters had the privilege of participating in this program. Lela Gutierrez and Eulogia Naranjo of Santa Clara Pueblo, Maria Martinez of San Ildefonso, and Agrapino Quintana of Cochiti were the makers of pottery which was placed in the newly constructed National Park Service Regional Headquarters building in Santa Fe.

1936: OLD ART IN NEW FORMS

Shapes in Pueblo pottery were rather stable when the vessels were functional, but styles in form did change gradually and these same styles were more or less general throughout the entire Pueblo area. However, people are people no matter what period they may occupy—undoubtedly there were potters in the 1880s, the 1890s, the 1900s, the 1910s, and the 1920s who dominated the scene in any pottery-making community. There were those who excelled in the art. There were those who set the style. This was certainly true in the 1930s.

The revival of pottery making in the 1930s was oriented to a buying public. To attract the buyer, shapes became those with which the buyer had long been familiar—tall necked vases, pottery ashtrays and cigarette boxes, candlesticks, delightfully modelled pottery animal bookends, and jars for lampbases.

As the potters learned to handle these new shapes skillfully the Indian Fair Committee admitted these innovations for judging in the annual competition for prizes at the Fair.

In an article sponsored by the New Mexico Association on Indian Affairs which appeared in the New Mexico Magazine, September 1936, it was stated "that mere imitation even of one's own ancestral art is stultifying and that if Indian native art is to survive it must be a growing thing, suitable for the time and circumstances in which it is made and it must be created out of the imagination of the individual craftsman, not merely a faithful reproduction of the work of his ancestors."

1920-1940: RESULTS OF THE REVIVAL

SAN JUAN.   In 1930 Regina Cata (Mrs. Eulogio Cata) organized a pottery study group at San Juan Pueblo with the intent of improving the quality of San Juan wares. Eight potters studied the

Cochiti bowl (top), and Tesuque double jar (bottom), typical of traditional forms and designs which influenced pottery made at New Mexico pueblos in the 1930s.

San Juan incised jars (above) which show two of the incising techniques developed at the pueblo during the early 1930s.

ancient potsherds of wares made at San Juan in earlier times and selected *Potsuwi'i Incised Ware* (1450-1500) as a basis for a contemporary pottery type. Decorative zones of geometric fine line patterns were incised on the walls of this ancient pottery. This decorative scheme was the one that the San Juan potters chose to use on the upper bodies of well-formed, polished tan jars and bowls. Generally the jars were tall, the shoulders high on the vessel, and the body walls had a fairly straight inward slant from the shoulder curve to the small base. Bowls were low and very wide mouthed with a pronounced outcurve between rim zone and wide base. This was a complete departure from early forms. On both jars and bowls the rim zones and underbodies were highly polished tan.

Experimentation with incising resulted in the technique being applied when the surface was quite damp, when the surface was dry, and even after the vessel had been fired. Each method produced its own distinctive visual impression.

Later in the period the traditional globular shape appeared once more, in combination with a tan incised decorative zone and

polished red rim zone and underbody. During the development of the fine line incised ware the making of polished black wares and polished red wares was continued in both traditional forms and non-traditional forms.

SANTA CLARA. Much experimentation in form and design was also taking place in Santa Clara during this period as the potters of this pueblo searched for new ideas.

One of the innovations at this time which had a reasonable amount of commercial success was a highly polished dark red ware with designs in muted light colors (pastel red, blue-grey, various shades of tan and ochre) outlined in stark white—all with a matte surface. Geometric designs were most prevalent but floral patterns and even realistic "scenes" were made. Santa Clara potters produced this ware extensively for about two decades. Although more of this type was made at Santa Clara, other Tewa pueblos (Tesuque, San Ildefonso) also produced some. Plates, globular jars, even animalitos were decorated in this color scheme.

Creations of the innovative Santa Clara potters during the 1920-1940 period (above, and top of opposite page).

Carving designs on the surface of the vessel (intaglio) was another innovation which caught the fancy of potters during this period. Usually the designs were in a well-defined band around the vessel. When the finished jar or bowl was red the background or cut out area was buff colored or sometimes a light red. When the vessel was smudged in the firing process the background was matte black. This design technique gained great popularity by 1940.

Lela and Van Gutierrez, a wife and husband team of Santa Clara potters, tested many ideas. But only when they developed a decorative scheme featuring earth colors on a matte background did they achieve one which was an enduring success. Bold curvilinear designs on a neutral tan or beige became the base for a new Santa Clara style.

The matte black on polished black style perfected earlier by Julian Martinez of San Ildefonso was produced in 1927 in Santa Clara for the first time.

Animalitos were still popular with potter and buyer. In defense of animalitos, they were molded with a minimum of detail but with a great deal of subtle charm and visual appeal.

SAN ILDEFONSO.   The process for producing matte black design areas on a polished black surface, which Julian Martinez was rapidly perfecting, began to attract a great deal of attention during the early years of this period. By 1940 the black-on-black ware was a well established design style. Designs were generally confined to bands which were placed on the upperbody of jars and low globular bowls, and as an all-over ornamentation on the interior of shallow bowls or platters. Geometric elements, both angular and curvilinear, were featured in either polished or matte, design schemes.

San Ildefonso jar illustrating the style of matte black designs on a polished black surface produced by Maria and Julian Martinez in the 1920-1940 period.

It was during this period that conformity of shape as an identifying feature for San Ildefonso pottery became no longer valid. Since most of the potters at this pueblo were working in the new design style by the end of the period the need for individual variation was met by diversity of form.

As the popularity of the black-on-black wares increased, the popularity of the polychrome wares, favored in the early 1900s, decreased until they were nearly forgotten.

During the first five years of the Southwest Indian Fair, Maria Martinez, Tonita Roybal, and Susana Aguilar were consistent prize winners. All three of these ladies eventually gained fame that was well deserved. In 1922 Maria won the Special Prize for a *new style* in decorated ware. Although there is no positive record of the specific ware which won the prize, it can be assumed that undoubtedly it was the black-on-black style.

Midway during this period carved wares were introduced at San Ildefonso by Rose Gonzales, who went on to earn great recognition for her work in this technique.

In 1925 Maria began to sign her name to her work. This was an event which had a profound effect on the pottery making world. Before too many years had passed most potters were also signing their work and collectors were not only acquiring pottery but they were "collecting" potters as well. Interest in the potters' private lives, biographical data, was manifest among collectors, both professional and amateur. This was both boon and bore for the potters, but it became an accepted practice and was, of course, a good one.

Tesuque.   In the 1920s the then recently developed "show-card" colors, or poster paint, was discovered by Tesuque potters. This was just the thing to make anything to which it was applied

Another vessel made by Maria and Julian Martinez in the 1920-1940 era, typical of the matte black design on polished black surface style they originated.

Miniature figures from Tesuque made during the 1920s (above and opposite page).

"look Indian" to the curio seeker—so Tesuque supplied "Indian" curios in great quantity. Every bright hue in the color spectrum was visible on salt and pepper shakers, small figurines, canoes, miniature jars and bowls, and the list could go on and on. The paint was applied after firing (if the piece was fired at all) and consequently was rather impermanent.

In 1926 Martin Vigil was a prize winner at the Southwest Indian Fair. He went on to recognition as the maker of charming miniature figures depicting the every day activities of Pueblo life.

SANTO DOMINGO.   During the early part of this period there was a continuation of small, poorly made tourist ware to be sold by the

Two vessels above are Santo Domingo wares from the 1920-1940 period.

roadside (a style which had developed during the early 1900s apart from the more traditional wares still being made). But later in the period there was an improvement in the quality of the tourist ware. Designs at this later date began to include birds, plant forms, and animals, with accents of red, much more than ever before. The potential for sales seemed to be greater when these design elements were used. These design schemes were also used on the larger well made jars in the typical Santo Domingo form with flaring rim, constricted neck and widest diameter somewhat above the mid-zone.

Also during these two decades experimentation with black-on-black ware was going on. Expertise in this technique at Santo

63

Cochiti jar (top) from the 1920-1940 period, and Santa Ana jar (bottom) produced late in the same era.

Domingo never did reach the perfection achieved by potters of the Tewa pueblos to the north.

The forms of these two styles (the polychrome and the black-on-black) were less "junky" than that of a decade earlier. Tall vases, jars with restricted necks, bowls with strap handles, and small plates were seen more frequently.

COCHITI.   In the search for a new type of saleable ware one of the Cochiti potters broke with tradition completely. In 1930, pottery with a highly polished red surface and matte white decorations made its appearance. The ware was well done, but it evidently didn't catch on because very little is known about it.

The traditional black-on-cream household wares of Cochiti and the figurines, produced in ever smaller sizes, were being made in moderate quantities during these two decades. But Cochiti drums were becoming even more popular.

SANTA ANA.   The sharp decline in pottery making at Santa Ana was not interrupted during this period of revival for most of the northern New Mexico pueblos, and by the end of this period Santa Ana pottery was almost a thing of the past. In fact, by 1940 there was only one Santa Ana woman who was working in the potter's art, and what she produced was made for Santa Ana.

At this time residents of Santa Ana were content to trade with Zia for their household wares which were superior to their own.

ZIA.   Along the Jemez River Zia women were the only ones who were actively producing pottery at this time. Their wares were much in demand by the people of the nearby pueblos who needed the thin walled, high fired, attractive jars in their household activities. The jars were acquired through trade.

The form of these popular Zia vessels had not changed substantially but the designs became basically geometric, undoubtedly reflecting the encouragement given in 1923-1924 to use the older native Zia designs.

ISLETA.   Although there is no record for the 1920-1940 period of the type of Isleta pottery exhibited during the first few years of the Southwest Indian Fair, there remains the fact that five Isleta potters were prize winners—so there must have been some competition within the pueblo. Also, it is known that during these two decades Isleta potters were selling Laguna-type polychrome wares at the Santa Fe Railroad station in Albuquerque.

LAGUNA.   With the building of cross-country highways Laguna found a ready made market for inexpensive, small wares made for quick sale to the tourists who travelled U.S. 66. The jars and bowls were imperfectly formed, designs and colors were pleasing variations of the traditional patterns but were large and very simple—on which very little time was needed to be spent.

ACOMA.   During the period when pottery had a limited production throughout the entire Pueblo world, pottery making at Acoma continued with moderate vigor. Pottery with interlocking swirls and stepped elements (both solid and hachured in various arrangements)—plant forms and birds featured with the use of yellow, orange, and dark red as decorative accents continuing from the past—was still being made. Whatever variations that were seen at this time were apparently limited only by the individual potter's designing ability.

Instead of a *revival* at Acoma, a time of change was taking place. The first evidence of non-traditional concepts at Acoma came

Well-designed jar from Zia of the type continuously produced from 1920-1940 (top), and an example of the hastily made Laguna ware available on roadsides during that period (bottom).

65

Pottery made at Acoma during the 1920-1940 period illustrates the diversity of design (top and center), and inspiration from the Hopi country (bottom).

during the 1930s with the use by some potters of the several typical Acoma design schemes depicted in unusual color combinations. Combinations of a red-orange slip as background for black and grey designs, and orange-red used with geometric patterns which had always been exclusively black-on-white, were two very short lived styles that appeared.

During this period some potters sought inspiration from archaeological sources to bring about a distinctive style for their Acoma pottery. Geometric and fine line patterns began to be seen much more often.

The brilliant white slip which had always been used by Acoma women was still one of the identifying features of pottery made there during this period. In spite of the great popularity of the stark black-on-white patterns, the early traditional polychrome designs never entirely lost their appeal for many Acoma potters and were still sought by many collectors and casual buyers.

ZUNI.   The intricate fine line designs, the little red birds in a band around the jars, the deer with the heart-line and the elaborate rosette, all in panels both vertical and horizontal, which had always been a part of the design schemes of Zuni made pottery, continued with very little change until the late 1930s. The volume of pottery produced was small, a trend begun in the early 1900s, but it continued to be well made, well designed and well fired. At last pottery making stopped, except for small and large owl figures, because jewelry making dominated the Zuni scene.

4 · INDIAN SELF-DIRECTION

During the period when the non-Indian was endeavoring to help the Indian to better his life through the making of better pottery—and realize his potential as a master craftsman—the hope was, of course, that the Indian would also realize his potential as an independent human being in American society.

Just as the program to bring about improvements in pottery was rewarding to all concerned with it, so was the ultimate result—the dawning of the day when the Indian took his place in the twentieth century as an individual capable of directing his own destiny.

1940s: VITAL CHANGES

After the search for new concepts in pottery designing and the "revival" of the 1930s, the very active potters, having found the *open sesame* to the commercial world, were busy producing wares that sold well and were busy establishing their reputations as the makers of the pottery which collectors should include in their holdings.

Then came World War II. This had its effect on Pueblo homes just as it did on other homes throughout the world. The percentage of Pueblo young people who served in the Armed Forces was high. Pottery making became more or less static; the vigorous search for the new and different slowed.

The three institutions that had been so active in helping the potters—giving encouragement and finding ways to make it all possible—also experienced changes.

Although the New Mexico Association on Indian Affairs continued to keep its protective eye on the Pueblo people it had also taken up the challenge of Navajo tribal affairs in financial matters and education. The Association also kept in close touch with all the Indian youth who were serving their country.

The Laboratory of Anthropology and the Indian Arts Fund, dependent on financial support from interested individuals, found that the wartime economy was not adequate for their needs. It took its toll. The Laboratory was unable to continue as before and in 1947 it became a part of the Museum of New Mexico. The Indian Arts Fund marked time until it could once again resume its program of collecting.

1950: YOUNGER GENERATION IS INTERESTED IN POTTERY

Five years after the disrupting war years were over it was reported in the minutes of the Indian Arts Fund's Annual Meeting, July 17, 1950, that students at the Santa Fe Indian School had been studying the pottery collections at the Laboratory of Anthropology. So—a new generation of potters was looking toward the future.

1962: INSTITUTE OF AMERICAN INDIAN ARTS ESTABLISHED

The impact of this event on traditional Pueblo pottery making was felt not at all. Ceramic students were and still are taught the

Vessels from Santa Clara (opposite page), Zia (top), Zuni (center), and Acoma (bottom), illustrating the diversity of design and form that had come about by the start of the 1940-1976 era.

69

Pottery of Santa Clara (top and center) and San Ildefonso from the 1940-1976 period.

use of the wheel and kiln-firing, a bonafide process for producing art wares, but not as yet popular with Pueblo potters.

This technique may in time affect traditional pottery making, for even now some stoneware may be seen for sale at the Santa Fe Indian Market.

1960-1976:   CHANGE TOWARD SELF-DIRECTION

In the 1960s and 1970s pottery making in the New Mexico pueblos was well established, gaining momentum and creating a vigorous worldwide interest. Competitive Indian craft-art shows and markets were held more frequently and in many more places, with the number increasing every year.

Competition was keen among the potters to produce prize winning wares and equally keen among collectors to acquire these prize winning wares. Although the demand for pottery was high, the prices rising, and production yields were rewarding, the potters and other Indian artist-craftsmen desired improvement in their crafts, needed more established and dependable sales outlets and more constant exposure to a public so anxious to acquire the Pueblo wares.

The Indians themselves took the initiative during these decades in gaining the help they needed. The Eight Northern Indian Pueblos Council led the way. All crafts were considered in the new movement and much was accomplished for the benefit of all craftsmen. Although pottery making was already well established, much was also gained for the potters from the efforts of the other artists-craftsmen to become independent in *their* own way.

Several very positive actions took place as a result of this determination on the part of the Indian community.

Indian Artists-Craftsmen Seminars Scheduled, 1968

The purpose of the seminars was to give information and training in business techniques and encouragement to form co-operative organizations.

Oke Oweenge Arts and Crafts Co-op Established, 1968

Much work and planning took place slowly at first but in 1970 study groups from the Co-op, under the direction of Mrs. Geronima C. Montoya, began regularly scheduled visits to the Anthropology Division of the Museum of New Mexico to examine and study the collections items—to learn techniques and record the traditional designs of the northern New Mexico pueblos. Remodeling an existing building in San Juan Pueblo for the Co-op headquarters was begun in 1972 and within the year it was a going concern. The Grand Opening took place at the First Artist and Craftsman Show held in 1973.

Eight Northern Pueblos Annual Artist and Craftsman Show, 1973

After much consideration, the Eight Northern Indian Pueblos Council (which includes the pueblos of Nambe, Pojoaque, Picuris, San Juan, San Ildefonso, Santa Clara, Taos, and Tesuque) sponsored the Eight Northern Indian Pueblos Annual Artist and Craftsman Show.

The first show (1973) was held at San Juan Pueblo, the second (1974) at San Ildefonso, the third (1975) at Pojoaque, and the fourth (1976) at Santa Clara. These competitive shows are staged for two days in the middle of July. The first two shows were juried by non-Indian individuals expert in Indian arts and crafts, but beginning with the third show Indian experts were called upon to

Zia Pueblo example from the 1940-1976 period.

71

Cochiti Pueblo pottery produced during the present era, a time of flourishing craftsmanship.

judge the work of their peers. Successful from the very beginning, these shows have increased phenomenally in size and popularity.

SANTO DOMINGO PUEBLO CRAFTS SHOW, 1975

Late in the summer of 1975 Santo Domingo Pueblo held the first annual Pueblo Crafts Show. All Pueblo craftsmen were invited to participate in exhibiting their crafts and many did. And so—another opportunity to present craft-arts to a potential buying public was established.

INDIAN MARKET AT SANTA FE, 1975

Although not Indian conceived or managed, the Indian Market in Santa Fe, sponsored by the Southwest Association on Indian Affairs (which is certainly Indian oriented) received its largest participation in all of its long history. All four sides of the Santa Fe Plaza were devoted to this remarkable display of Indian wares.

INDIAN PUEBLO CULTURAL CENTER, 1975

Incorporated in 1975 as an associated program of the All Indian Pueblo Council, the Indian Pueblo Cultural Center in Albuquerque will serve as a multi-use facility, conceived, owned, and operated by the Pueblo Indians of New Mexico. In concept it is oriented to advancing understanding and insuring preservation of Pueblo tradition and culture, and to providing economic and cultural benefits to the entire community.

The Center's activities include a living arts program, marketing and sales opportunities, a hallmark program to guarantee that each Pueblo Indian made product is genuine, a museum, and an educational program. As stated in the brochure issued soon after its inception, "The unifying spirit of the Indian Pueblo Cultural

Center will bring the people of all the Pueblos closer together as they encounter common problems and work toward achievement of common goals."

NORTHERN PUEBLO INDIAN ARTISANS GUILD, 1976

The Guild opened in January, 1976 at San Juan Pueblo. Its purposes are to establish a year-round sales outlet for Pueblo craftsmen, make available to the artisans raw materials for the production of saleable items, provide instruction in craft techniques, and to exhibit current wares.

Not only will a composite presentation of all crafts of the Northern Pueblos be available to the visitor and collector but a pottery collection representing Acoma, Zia, Cochiti and Santo Domingo will also be featured. Classes in pottery making will be in session often and visitors are invited to watch the processes of pottery making. Jewelry, paintings, Taos drums, and other handcrafts will compete in interest with the pottery displays.

1940-1976   POTTERY BECOMES ART

With money just not available for luxuries, with travel curtailed and with interest centered on so many other things during the war years, the demand for Indian pottery at that time and for a few years afterwards was very small. But time went by, travel limitations were lifted, and public interest in Indian craft work once again manifested.

Following trends begun before the war years, the traditional forms and designs, as trademarks of an entire pueblo, were no longer a part of Indian ceramic art, although schemes and coloration did generally reflect the tradition of the pueblo in which

Two examples of Zia Pueblo craftsmanship, made during the most recent period.

73

San Juan vessels of the new style and an earlier style, from the 1940-1976 period.

the individual potter practiced her or his art. The word *art* became more and more valid as the years went by—the potter became truly an artist in many, many instances.

SAN JUAN.   The incised wares developed at San Juan during the 1930s became well established in the next decades. Some potters preferred to produce the all-tan vessels and platters, while others featured a combination of incised patterns on a tan ground and highly polished red rims and underbodies.

Improvements and variations appeared. The incised lines were accented with white, red, and micaceous clay paints. The carving of some areas was also introduced.

Another decorative style was developed during this period which became very popular. In this, designs were accented with very low profile carving, and painted with white and several shades of red. Neck and underbody areas were a deep, highly polished red. Vessel shapes were diverse, some tall, some spherical. This design scheme appeared on small novelty items too. And each potter developed her own individual decorative pattern.

These two San Juan styles are still being made, although during the last ten or twelve years weaving, superb embroidery featuring traditional Pueblo designs on smartly tailored garments, and the carving of wooden dance figures fashioned in an expert stylistic manner, have captured the interest of many of the deft San Juan craft-artists.

SANTA CLARA.   Polished black carved ware became so popular during the 1950s, gaining momentum as time went by, that at the present moment most Santa Clara potters are not only capable of producing it but several are true masters at it. The *avanyu* (plumed serpent of Tewa legend) was and still is a design motif most favored by Santa Clara potters—and advisedly so, because with buyers it is also a favorite. The angular and curvilinear geometric patterns, if bold and well integrated, could be and were used by many potters very successfully, and in the hands of the experts were truly works of art in many instances.

The "bear paw" motif was adopted by Santa Clara potters in the early years of the twentieth century and since then it has become identified with Santa Clara. On a highly polished, well formed vessel it has great appeal. Innovative use of turquoise and silver, inlaid in highly polished black vessels, is now appearing at Santa Clara.

Santa Clara pottery making has been very successful and much of beauty has been produced there. Entire families (four generations in some families, such as in the Tafoya-Naranjo family) are active and expert in the art. Younger members of these families are producing exquisite miniature vessels decorated in a technique known as *sgraffito* (a form of carving), in polished black, red, and/or tan by means of a special type of firing. Two young men entered this field in the early 1970s and are excelling in the style.

The polychrome wares perfected by Lela and Van in the early 1900s continue to be produced by younger members of the Gutierrez family.

Animalitos at Santa Clara, begun as novelties so many, many years ago, have endured and endeared since their first appearance. Recently examples of them have stepped out of the novelty class and into the class of true sculpture. These are larger but have the subtle molding which minimizes detail but leaves the beholder with no doubt as to the animal depicted. This quality is superb.

The diversity of pottery making at Santa Clara is depicted in these three distinctly different design styles.

San Ildefonso polychrome closed jar produced in 1976.

SAN ILDEFONSO.   The black-on-black wares continued to be extremely popular through the entire 1940-1976 period to the present day. However, the imaginative, creative artists of San Ildefonso are not content to do the same thing over and over again for very long. Maria's son, Popovi Da, an excellent potter in his own right, began to experiment with a special firing technique to produce sienna-and-black two tone wares. This process was so successful in the 1950s from an artistic point of view that it became the basis for further adaptation by contemporary minded potters both at San Ildefonso and Santa Clara. Popovi also returned to the polychrome styles of an earlier day, producing extremely well-made, very "modern" vessels using traditional design motifs.

Until her recent retirement, Maria's family included four generations of active potters. The younger members of this family have produced exquisite sculpture, vessels featuring sgraffito, two-tone sienna-and-black, and turquoise inlay, with these techniques used singly or in combination.

In a later day, Blue Corn has successfully carried the polychrome concept into paths unthought of by other potters. With imagination and creative ability Blue Corn has produced many unusual pottery pieces. Other potters are following her lead.

The carved wares, begun earlier by Rose Gonzales, are still being produced by her and every vessel is a masterpiece. Rose's son prefers the challenge of the two-tone style, the sgraffito, the turquoise inlay.

TESUQUE.   The bright colored novelties decorated with poster paint in no way diminished as the years went by, but several potters tried valiantly to revive pottery made in the more traditional form with sedate, simple designs in black and red on a white or cream slip—and fired properly *after* the designs were put on. Not being pueblo-wide projects these efforts didn't attract much attention, but there are potters today who are still making efforts to return to the "old" style Tesuque pottery. And, poster paint has about run its course.

In the 1940s Manuel Vigil began to produce charming small figurines depicting the dancers who participated in Tesuque rituals, as well as figures which portrayed the people performing everyday tasks such as grinding corn, holding the baby, baking bread. In the late 1960s he turned his attention to depicting the Christian nativity, known locally as *nacimiento*. The figurines were clothed with fabrics suitable to their respective roles in the scene; the animals were modeled in realistic form but with very little detail, and much charm.

SANTO DOMINGO.   A few potters who were interested in producing wares comparable in form and design to the earlier traditional types continued to make a moderate quantity of pottery, yet they were lacking in the skill needed to produce vessels of the quality of those made by their Tewa neighbors to the north.

Santo Domingo had turned to jewelry. The craftsmen of this pueblo were especially capable of creating exceptional heishi (the small disk beads made of shell) and turquoise disk beads—and many individuals were and are actively engaged in this art. Many more engaged in fabricating novelty jewelry items for quick sale. Unfortunately, pottery making was much less remunerative for the craftsmen of Santo Domingo.

COCHITI.   By the late 1950s there were only three potters who were producing the good, old style Cochiti wares. However, figurines with great appeal were being produced in greater

Miniature Tesuque dance figures (top) and a simple but very striking design style made at Santo Domingo during the 1940-1976 period.

77

quantity. A new type of figure made its appearance—the storyteller doll—and its popularity was instantaneous. The inventive potter featured an adult as the central focus in her composite figure, with charming children swarming all over the storyteller much as any children do when a "story" is about to be told. Its inventor, Helen Cordero, has never been able to produce them fast enough. This form of art has captured the imagination of other Cochiti potters.

SANTA ANA.   For many years no pottery was produced at Santa Ana. Then in 1973, with the organizational expertise of Miss Nancy Winslow and funds from the Save the Children Federation, Santa Ana women who were interested in reviving pottery making studied pottery collections in the Museum of New Mexico and other museums, learned the techniques from clay gathering to firing, and were instructed in pricing and merchandising. The project resulted in a successful program in pottery production of contemporary saleable wares based on traditional form and design. Women at Santa Ana now have an ideal method for supplementing family income.

ZIA.   Silver was one of the metals which were "frozen" during World War II. The Zias, ingenious potters all, began making *pottery buttons* with Zia polychrome geometric designs and birds as decorations. These had a diameter of about one and one-half inches, were extremely attractive, and in 1942 and 1943 were used on leather jackets manufactured in Albuquerque. Of course, when silver was once more available these delightful, impractical objects were seen no more.

As younger Zia potters joined the ranks of the ceramic artists, design changes of course came about. There was a return to the

Storyteller figurine from Cochiti, 1975.

older design schemes of the double zoned red meander and the birds. The rounded, rather static red realistic birds became streamlined birds, painted black, streaking through the air on black hachured wings. Dark brown and red designs on a stark white background were crisp and very neat, with a most contemporary appearance. As time advanced small curio vessels were made but always with the artistic expertise of Zia potters—nothing junky was ever produced.

JEMEZ.   Over the years since the 1920s Jemez potters have experimented with many materials and techniques—kiln fired commercial colors and glazes, poster paint and acrylics.

Also over the years several potters have seriously attempted to bring about a move toward (or perhaps back to) the traditional use of red clay paint and *guaco* (a vegetal paint which fires black) in designs. But their efforts have not been successful. However, today's designs done in strong tones of brown on a tan ground with geometric patterns are fairly well established.

One potter is making the most delightful miniature vessels which are very small—measuring less than one inch in height. These do display the white clay slip with traditional red and black geometric design schemes.

ISLETA.   As poster paint came to several pueblos, so it eventually came to Isleta during the 1950s. Soon after that Isleta pottery once again became rather rare.

In the 1970s there was a revival of sorts. One family in Isleta is using the commercially produced pre-formed undecorated ware available to hobbyists and decorating it with expertly conceived non-traditional designs. However, a member of one of Isleta's well

Four fine examples of Zia pottery from the 1940-1976 period.

79

Typical examples of Acoma pottery produced during the 1940-1976 era (above, and opposite page).

known pottery making families (Chewiwi) is now making pottery in the traditional way and decorating it with the Laguna type elements which by now could be termed "traditional" as well.

LAGUNA.　　During the early years of the post-1940 period pottery making was abandoned at Laguna, but in 1972, under the competent direction of Nancy Winslow and funds from the Manpower Development and Training Act, a program of the type which was carried out at Santa Ana was initiated at Laguna. The Laguna program took place a year earlier than the one at Santa Ana, and was the pattern for the one at Santa Ana. It had been proven that such endeavor could be successful, establishing a new home industry in the community.

ACOMA.　　Lucy Lewis had been making pottery in the early 1900s when she was a child, but in the 1950s she changed the whole design scheme of Acoma produced pottery. Working with the traditional Acoma designs which were so popular for so many years—the elaborate patterns which included curvilinear and angular geometric elements, fine line hachure, plant forms and birds in black, and red-orange and yellow on a stark white background—Lucy had perfected her forms and design execution, and had gained some recognition in this style by the 1950s.

But during the early 1950s she began using the Zuni deer with the heart-line (with the permission of Zuni Pueblo), and later in the 1950s she introduced the fine line patterns which were adaptations of ancient Mimbres design elements and other prehistoric decorative motifs. Although Lucy is famous for her fine line concept in design, it is interesting to note that she has never completely abandoned the traditional polychrome styles.

Marie Z. Chino, who was in the ranks of the prize winners at the first Southwest Indian Fair in 1922, had been producing an ornate black-on-white pattern based on prehistoric designs. The pattern included interlocking scrolls and geometric units with fine line hachure. She had done this for several years before Lucy Lewis began to feature the fine line concept as an all over pattern, so expertly executed that it had the quality of an optical illusion.

This contemporary version of an old style was ready made for Marie Chino. She and Lucy became friendly competitors, which benefitted the image of Acoma pottery immeasurably. The children and grandchildren of these two ladies are now active in pottery making, as are the children and grandchildren of several other noted Acoma potters of earlier years.

ZUNI.   Two years ago it was reported that Daisy Hooie (a descendant of Nampeyo, the famous Hopi potter) was teaching the Zuni women to once again make pottery. Obviously, the appeal and satisfaction of pottery making is still felt in a pueblo with a heritage of superb pottery form and design, even though ceramic art has not been a part of Zuni culture for many, many years.

*   *   *

Pottery making is truly a constant tradition in the New Mexico pueblos and it is to be hoped that it remains so. But considering the artistic talent of the makers, changes will inevitably come about because the artist must ever explore new paths.

The design and form of Pueblo pottery is expected to become ever more exciting.

APPENDIX

Suggested Reading

BOOKS:

Bunzel, Ruth L.
    The Pueblo Potter: A Study of Creative Imagination in Primitive Art.
    Columbia University Contributions to Anthropology No. VIII, New
    York, 1929.

Chapman, Kenneth M.
    The Pottery of San Ildefonso Pueblo. School of American Research
    and University of New Mexico Press, Albuquerque, 1970.

Chapman, Kenneth M.
    The Pottery of Santo Domingo Pueblo. Memoirs of the Laboratory of
    Anthropology, Vol. I, Santa Fe, 1953.

Fewkes, J. Walter
    Ancient Zuni Pottery. Putnam Anniversary Volume, G. E. Stechert
    and Company, New York, 1909.

Guthe, Carl E.
    Pueblo Pottery Making: A Study at the Village of San Ildefonso.
    Department of Archaeology, Phillips Academy, Yale, Andover,
    Massachusetts, 1925.

Harlow, Francis H., and John V. Young
    Contemporary Pueblo Indian Pottery. Museum of New Mexico Press,
    Santa Fe, 1965.

Harlow, Francis H.
    *Historic Pueblo Indian Pottery: Painted Jars and Bowls of the Period
    1600-1900.* Museum of New Mexico Press, Santa Fe, 1970.

Harlow, Francis H.
> *Matte-Paint Pottery of the Tewa, Keres and Zuni Pueblos.* Museum of New Mexico Press, Santa Fe, 1973.

Lambert, Marjorie
> *Pueblo Indian Pottery: Materials, Tools and Techniques.* Museum of New Mexico Press, Popular Series Pamphlet No. 5, Santa Fe, 1966.

Lange, Charles H.
> *Cochiti: A New Mexico Pueblo, Past and Present.* University of Texas Press, Austin, 1959.

LeFree, Betty
> *Santa Clara Pottery Today.* School of American Research and the University of New Mexico Press, Albuquerque, 1975.

Maxwell Museum
> *Seven Families in Pueblo Pottery.* Maxwell Museum of Anthropology, University of New Mexico, Albuquerque, 1974.

Tanner, Clara Lee
> *Southwest Indian Craft Arts.* University of Arizona Press, Tucson, 1968.

Wormington, H. M., and Arminta Neal
> *The Story of Pueblo Pottery.* Museum Pictorial No. 2, Museum of Natural History, Denver, 1951.

ARTICLES:

Chapman, Kenneth M.
> Post-Spanish Pueblo Pottery. *Art and Archaeology,* Vol. 23, No. 5, Washington, 1927.

Chapman, Kenneth M.
> Bird Forms in Zuni Pottery Decoration. *El Palacio,* Vol. 24, No. 2, January 14, 1928.

Chapman, Kenneth M.

Roadside Shopping. *New Mexico Magazine*, Vol. 14, No. 6, June, 1936.

Dietrich, Margaretta S.

Old Art in New Forms. *New Mexico Magazine*, Vol. 14, No. 9, September, 1936.

Ellis, Florence H.

On Distinguishing Laguna from Acoma Polychrome. *El Palacio*, Vol. 73, No. 3, Autumn, 1966.

Olman, Minnie

Lucy Lewis: Acoma's Versatile Potter. *El Palacio*, Vol. 75, No. 2, Summer, 1968.

Schroeder, Gail P.

San Juan Pottery: Methods and Incentives. *El Palacio*, Vol. 71, No. 1, Spring, 1964.

Spinden, Herbert J.

The Making of Pottery at San Ildefonso Pueblo. *The American Museum Journal*, Vol. 11, The American Museum of Natural History, New York, 1911.

Table of Pottery Dimensions

The following list gives the *height* (except where indicated) of each of the over 150 examples of Pueblo pottery that accompany the text.

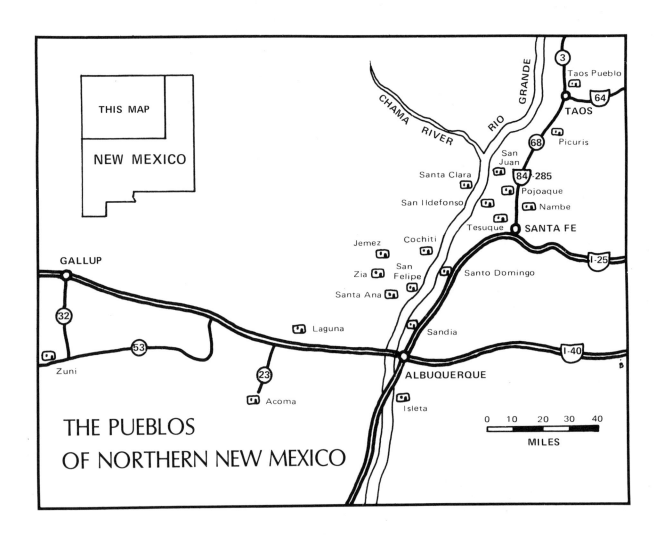

THIS MAP

NEW MEXICO

CHAMA RIVER

RIO GRANDE

3

Taos Pueblo

64

TAOS

68 Picuris

San Juan

84-285

Santa Clara

Pojoaque

San Ildefonso

Nambe

Tesuque

SANTA FE

Jemez

Cochiti

I-25

Zia

San Felipe

Santo Domingo

Santa Ana

32

GALLUP

Laguna

Sandia

53

I-40

23

Zuni

ALBUQUERQUE

Acoma

Isleta

0 10 20 30 40

MILES

THE PUEBLOS
OF NORTHERN NEW MEXICO